RUSSIAN SECURITY STRATEGY UNDER PUTIN: U.S. AND RUSSIAN PERSPECTIVES

U.S. INTERESTS IN THE NEW EURASIA

R. Craig Nation

RUSSIA'S THREAT PERCEPTION AND STRATEGIC POSTURE

Dmitri Trenin

November 2007

This publication is a work of the U.S. Government as defined in Title 17, United States Code, Section 101. As such, it is in the public domain, and under the provisions of Title 17, United States Code, Section 105, it may not be copyrighted.

*****

The views expressed in this report are those of the authors and do not necessarily reflect the official policy or position of the Department of the Army, the Department of Defense, or the U.S. Government. This report is cleared for public release; distribution is unlimited.

*****

Comments pertaining to this report are invited and should be forwarded to: Director, Strategic Studies Institute, U.S. Army War College, 122 Forbes Ave, Carlisle, PA 17013-5244.

*****

All Strategic Studies Institute (SSI) publications are available on the SSI homepage for electronic dissemination. Hard copies of this report also may be ordered from our homepage. SSI's homepage address is: *www.StrategicStudiesInstitute.army.mil.*

*****

FOREWORD

The two papers grouped together here were delivered at the Strategic Studies Institute's annual strategy conference for 2007. As the theme of the conference was global security challenges to the United States and proceeded on a region by region basis, these papers were delivered during the session devoted to security challenges issuing from what is now called Eurasia, i.e., to a large degree the former Soviet Union. The authors illustrate the degree to which great power rivalry in Eurasia has become a major security issue and source of growing Russo-American tensions. Whereas Dr. R. Craig Nation lays out some of the fundamental macro-strategic issues of this rivalry and U.S. goals in Eurasia, as well as the consequences of Russian resistance to Western and American pressures, Dr. Dmitri Trenin emphasizes the growing intensity of Russian threat perceptions.

Inasmuch as the conference aimed to heighten understanding of present and forthcoming security challenges, these points concerning the centrality of context and the mutually interactive nature of Russo-American security agendas and dialogues are of great importance in helping us grasp the tenor of our times.

DOUGLAS C. LOVELACE, JR.
Director
Strategic Studies Institute

SUMMARY

Increasingly, the armed forces and a vision of security as emphasizing hard rather than soft security have come to the fore in Moscow's national security policy process. Due to this institutionally-driven vision, Russia sees itself facing increasing military-political and strategic threats all along its frontiers. Recent Russian policies reflect that perception and Moscow's adaptation to it. We may think this threat perception to be misguided, even bizarrely misconceived, given our own beliefs about what American policy is and what its goals are. Nevertheless, the strongest forces in the Russian policy community have bought into that vision and have made policy accordingly.

Therefore, the key point that readers should take as they read these papers together is that Russian and American perspectives and policies are mutually interactive. They do not take place in a strategic vacuum devoid of all context, and develop to a considerable degree in response to the other side's activities and rhetoric. Neither we nor Russia can act in disregard of the fact that our actions have consequences and that other state actors in Eurasia, as elsewhere, also have a vote in shaping the context of international affairs and in the day-to-day conduct of U.S. and Russian national security policy.

U.S. INTERESTS IN THE NEW EURASIA

R. Craig Nation

Mysteries of Eurasia.

According to the geopolitical theory of Sir Halford Mackinder, control of the Eurasian heartland, with its "incalculably great" resource base and central strategic location, was the key to global leadership.[1] The "problem" of Eurasia was resolved historically by the combination of Russian power and backwardness. The traditional Russian state imposed a kind of order within the vast region, but remained too underdeveloped to threaten traditional balances of power.

The Russian empire sought to define itself as a national complex that embraced the Russian lands and their border regions within a shared civilizational space with a common destiny. The Russian state tradition, together with Russian language and culture, played the role of unifiers, providing the physical and spiritual force of what commentators like Nikolai Berdiaev and Petr Struve called the "Russian Idea." These theorists argued that Russia's integrative role in Eurasia was a foundation of its national identity. This was a Russia that encompassed "all those who participate in Russian culture" and was part of, but also distinct from, the culture of the West.[2] "The Russian people is not purely European, and it is not purely Asiatic," wrote Berdiaev. "Russia is a complete section of the world, and within the Russian soul two principles are always engaged in strife—the Eastern and Western."[3]

The challenge of alternative sources of order in a Eurasia lacking a strong Russian state capable of serving as *Ordnungsmacht* was posed by the breakdown that accompanied the outcome of World War I, but was temporarily resolved by the triumph of Soviet power. The disappearance of the Union of Soviet Socialist Republics (USSR) and the demise of the Cold War system that sanctioned Soviet control over the Eurasian land mass posed the challenge once again. For some observers, the Soviet collapse was an illustration that the imperial idea itself was fatally flawed.[4] In Russia the events of 1991 were sometimes interpreted as a reincarnation of the breakdown of 1917, a confirmation of the decadence of the imperial tradition and "a demonstration . . . that the 'collapse' of the Russian Empire in 1917 was by no means coincidental."[5] For others it was the chiliastic pretense of Soviet communism that had been exposed. In either case, the coherence that Russian and Soviet authority once imposed upon the heartland seemed to have disappeared forever.

The enthusiastic association of the new Russian leadership of Boris Yeltsin with the leading western powers, and the United States in particular, briefly seemed to be a watershed in Russian history. Deprived at a stroke of its imperial inheritance, submitted to the constraints of democratic governance, and exposed to the discipline of the world market, Russia was presumed to be committed to a process of "transition" that would lead it inexorably toward some variant of the western model.[6] Abandonment of the imperial legacy and the associated dynamic of expansionism was considered to be particularly important. Russia's critics defined autocratic governance and expansionism as complementary aspects of the Russian state tradition—a tradition "that insisted on strong, centralized authority, unconstrained either by law or parliament" in search of "security through constant expansion."[7] The break up of the Soviet Union was an opportunity for Russia to escape from the demons of its past. Only by shedding its imperial pretense, accepting the costs of dismantling centralized control, and cultivating horizontal ties between citizens as a foundation for an autonomous civil society, could Russia hope to put paid to its messianic traditions and realize the goal of joining the West.[8] This meant abandoning the aspiration to cultivate a distinctive Eurasian space and identity as a foundation for national power. The choice between "Russian national state" and "Eurasian empire" was posed as a fateful one. "Fundamentally," wrote Zbigniew Brzezinski, "the political struggle within Russia is over whether Russia will be a national and increasingly European state or a distinctively Eurasian and once again an imperial state."[9]

Rather than serving as a prelude to a fundamental reorientation, however, the first phase of post-communist transition led directly to a severe economic depression, a breakdown of civic order and public morale, and a widespread perception of international defeat and humiliation. The formula "democratization, market economy, and the rule of law," far from imposing a new sense of meaning based upon the material civilization of the West, created what was widely felt to be an anarchical void in which Russia's entire civilization legacy was swallowed up — a "phase of tragic schism and anarchy" in the words of A. N. Sakharov.[10]

One consequence was the revival of the concept of Eurasia as a foundation for the Russian national idea. Already in 1993 a new Russian Military Doctrine proclaimed the Commonwealth of Independent States (CIS) area a region of Russian "vital interests," and the Russian Federation's new Foreign Policy Concept identified the former USSR as a region of Russian "special responsibility."[11] Under foreign minister Evgenii Primakov, cultivating a Russian sphere of influence in the post-Soviet space was defined as a national commitment of the highest order.[12] This concept has remained intact under the administration of Vladimir Putin. A recently released survey of Russian foreign policy priorities states baldly that developing close relations with the new independent states of post-Soviet Eurasia "is the first priority of Russian foreign policy."[13] Putin advisors have articulated a vision of Eurasian order based upon a division of responsibilities between an enlarged European Union (EU) as a dominant force in the West and Russia as a renewed hegemonic leader in Eurasia.[14]

Whether Russia will become a European nation in the sense implied by Brzezinski is not a question that Russian policymakers are in a position to answer. But there is a consensus that if Russia is to interact with Europe and the West on a basis of equality, it must use Eurasia as a base. In current Russian foreign policy discourse, the concept of Eurasia does not evoke the mystical source of cultural affiliation and physical power popular on the far-right of the political spectrum.[15] Nor does it imply the goal of some kind of Eurasian Union as a spiritual successor to the USSR.[16] But it does refer to the geographical context within which Russia's most important foreign policy goals must be pursued.

Washington has consistently opposed Moscow's interference in the affairs of the new independent states on its borders and sought to resist any kind of imperial revival. Consolidation of the sovereignty of the new independent states and preservation of the post-Soviet geopolitical status quo in the name of "geopolitical pluralism" remains a foundation for regional policy. The U.S. State Department/U.S. Agency for International Development *Joint Strategic Plan* for the years 2007-2012, for example, describes aggressive Russian policies toward its neighbors as "a major challenge."[17] These priorities are not likely to change, and a competitive relationship with a more dynamic Russian Federation will be an unavoidable result. At the same time, it is important not to exaggerate Russian capacity. Despite its impressive revival, the Russian Federation remains a troubled and potentially fragile polity whose ambition may well come to exceed its grasp. Blocking Russian imperial revival is a foundation of U.S. Eurasian policy, but it is important to think systematically about the consequences of success. What kind of Eurasian regional order will emerge in the absence of Russia as "ordering" force? What other U.S. interests are at play in this vast world region, and what kind of policies can most effectively secure them?

The concept of Eurasia is used in an inconsistent way within U.S. policy circles. The U.S. State Department maintains a Bureau of European and Eurasian Affairs parallel with a Bureau of Central and South Asian Affairs. The U.S. Defense Department's European Command Area of Responsibility includes "Eurasia" as a constituent part, parallel with a Central Command including former Soviet Central Asia. In both of these configurations, Europe, the greater Middle East, and Inner Asia are set apart—the substance of what is referred to as Eurasia amounts to little more than the Russian Federation and a handful of its weaker neighbors. Western analysts have consistently sought to assert that Eurasianism poses a false choice for contemporary Russia, whose post-communist destiny is still seen to lie in association with a wider West.[18] If we could realize the old Cold War vision of a unified security community stretching from Vancouver to Vladivostok, this perception might be a fair one. Unfortunately, it has become clear that the Russian Federation cannot and will not be assimilated into the Euro-Atlantic community. Russia's relations with Europe are troubled, and an EU in the grip of enlargement fatigue is not about to contemplate overtures to Muscovy. The case for including Russia as a full member of the new North Atlantic Treaty Organization (NATO) can be compelling, but it is also unrealistic. In fact, what is described as "Eurasia" in much of U.S. foreign policy analysis equates to a kind of limbo to which Russia has been willfully consigned as a consequence of what might be construed as a policy of exclusion. This limited vision does not correspond to the new strategic realities of the Eurasian region in an age of globalization, where the exclusion of important national players will not be an option. Nor does it correspond to the changing character of Eurasia itself, and the kind of strategic issues that it poses.

The new Eurasia is a geographical complex that includes the Russian Federation as an important actor, but is no longer defined either by the geopolitical fault lines of the Cold War or the weight of a reemerging Russian imperial tradition. Russia's aspiration to reassert itself as a force in the region may have some prospect of success, but attempts at dominion are bound to fail. In outline, the new Eurasia is best understood as a truncated version of Mackinder's World-Island, including Eurasia proper (with its European appendage), the greater Middle East along the southern flank, the inner Asian region including post-Soviet Central Asia as well as Afghanistan, Iran, and Pakistan, and significant parts of South and

East Asia.[19] Strategic linkages in sectors of seminal importance (energy, strategic lines of communication, global terrorism, and great power rivalry) allow us to define the region as a coherent strategic space where the United States has important interests at stake that can only be properly understood and pursued in their full geographical context.

These interests can be outlined, albeit somewhat schematically, as follows:

- Assuring access for ourselves and our allies to the energy resources of the region, which includes a critical mass of available global reserves;
- Defeating jihadist terrorism and addressing the root causes of the political and social disaffection that spawns it;
- Maintaining regional stability, including efforts to contain foci of instability along the "arc of crisis" on the region's southern flank;
- Managing the rise of an ambitious and increasingly powerful, but also potentially unstable China;
- Channeling the ambitions of other aspiring regional influentials and potential peer competitors, including a combative Iran and newly assertive India; and
- Promoting the democratic transition of the Russian Federation and on the basis of success in that endeavor working cooperatively with Russia in pursuit of mutual interests.

This list attempts to identify concrete issue areas that are defined by broad transnational patterns of association. They are unfolding in a new Eurasia, understood as a territorial complex characterized by strategic interlinkages but without an established basis for a stable regional order. The new Eurasia is a complex and diverse region, but it is not a mystery. It is a major strategic complex within which important U.S. interests are at stake. In the analysis that follows, some of the more salient of these interests will be explored.

Energy Security.

The United States is the world's largest energy consumer, and securing access to global supplies of energy resources is a vital national interest. It does not heavily depend upon Eurasian sources of hydrocarbons, but the role of Eurasia in world energy markets is increasingly important. Russia possesses up to 30 percent of known natural gas reserves and is the world's second oil producer after Saudi Arabia. It has large untapped reserves but requires investment and technological assistance to exploit them. Key U.S. allies in Europe depend heavily upon Russian supplies of hydrocarbons, and this dependency will inevitably increase. Europe presently takes 30 percent of its oil imports from Russia and 50 percent of its natural gas. If present trends continue, by 2030 up to 80 percent of Europe's energy needs will be supplied from Russian sources.[20] Russia is also the world's second consumer of energy after the United States.

The Russian Federation has a critical role to play assuring global energy security. Hydrocarbons are the crucial foundation for Russian national revival, and Putin has undertaken a series of initiatives to ensure that they are under firm state control. These initiatives have become a source of friction in relations between Russia and its Western partners. The destruction of

Yukos and abusive incarceration of its leader, Mikhail Khodokovskii, has become a kind of *cause célèbre* in the West and a symbol of Russia's purported authoritarian drift. Efforts to limit Western investment in the Russian oil and gas industry, the forced revocation of an Exxon-Mobile license to exploit the Sakhalin energy fields, and the collapse of other proposed joint ventures have generated mutual resentment. Accusations that Russia is now using energy transfers "as a weapon" in its efforts to impose new pricing structures in Ukraine and Belarus, with deleterious impact upon contracted supply to the EU market, are widespread, and Russia has reacted to criticism by floating the possibility of reorienting a portion of its energy exports toward the east.[21] Russia's effort to lay territorial claim to a portion of the Arctic seabed and its great hydrocarbon potential is only the most recent example of an assertive energy policy that is not afraid to throw down a gauntlet to the West.[22]

Expanded investment and technological cooperation could make the United States an attractive partner for Russia in the energy sector. For the time being, however, Washington has limited influence over Russia's domestic energy policy. The most disputed source of energy supply in the Eurasian region has been the Caspian Basin, where Washington has been quite successful in challenging Russia's privileged status.

By the mid-1990s, some U.S. estimates of the Caspian's oil potential reached 240 billion barrels, describing an El Dorado that rivaled the proven reserves of Saudi Arabia. Such expectations provided a powerful impetus for regional engagement. Commitments to opening up the region to Western influence and reducing dependency upon Moscow have been pursued consistently in spite of the fact that appraisals of the region's energy potential have been considerably reduced.[23] On July 21, 1997, Strobe Talbott described the Caspian region as "strategically vital," and this estimate continues to inspire U.S. regional policy.[24] Assuring access to Caspian resources has become an important strategic goal. Today, independent international sources such as British Petroleum estimate the Caspian's proven oil reserves at about 50 billion barrels and natural gas resources at 9 trillion cubic meters (4-5 percent of world reserves).[25] This potential does not come close to rivaling those of the Gulf region or the Russian Federation, but it ensures the Caspian region's status as an area of strategic interest.

Exploiting the region's potential has proven to be difficult due to its inherent instabilities and to the challenge of pipeline routing to bring resources from the land-locked Caspian into global markets.[26] At the moment of the collapse of the USSR in 1991, Moscow controlled all pipeline routes bringing oil and natural gas out of the Caspian basin. U.S. policy in the post-Soviet era has been directed toward facilitating the construction of multiple pipelines, allowing more equitable access that is not uniformly subject to Russian control. This agenda has become associated with a desire on the part of many regional states to lessen their degree of dependence upon Russia and encouraged leaning on the United States as an alternative source of foreign policy orientation. U.S. policy has also consistently sought to isolate Iran and contain its regional influence.

The result has been a "battle of pipelines" that is still underway. The completion of the Baku-Tbilisi-Ceyhan (BTC) main export pipeline (opened in the summer of 2006) represented a major challenge to Russia's position in the region, described by President George Bush as a "monumental achievement that opens a new era in the Caspian Basin's development."[27] A Baku-Tbilisi-Erzurum South Caucasus Pipeline project is also underway, directed at the Turkish market, with a spur through Greece that will direct some resources to Europe as well. A Kazakhstan Caspian Transportation System is planned to bring oil from the Kazakh Kashagan fields into the BTC pipeline network, and a "transport corridor" project seeks to bring natural gas from Turkmenistan and Kazakhstan into the European market by routes bypassing Russia. The United States has also expressed interest in a Turkmenistan-Afghanistan-Pakistan (TAP) natural gas pipeline, with possible Indian participation. The EU is sponsoring the construction of a Nabucco pipeline designed to bring natural gas from Turkey to Austria across Romania, Hungary, and Bulgaria, with a projected completion date of 2012. In the spring of 2006, during a state visit to Kazakhstan, U.S. Vice-President Richard Cheney chastened Moscow for seeking to monopolize energy trade in the former Soviet Union, and called upon Astana to opt for pipelines bypassing Russia.[28]

Russia has remained in a strong competitive position nonetheless. The Caspian Pipeline Consortium, of which Russia is an important member, takes about a third of Kazakhstan's oil production to the Russian Black Sea port of Novorossiisk, and Russia's Blue Stream link to Turkey supplies a large part of the Turkish natural gas market. In March 2007 Moscow signed an accord with Bulgaria and Greece to construct a Burgas-Alexandropoulis pipeline intended to rival the BTC and give Russia more direct access to the European market. In May 2007 Putin signed an accord with Turkmenistan and Kazakhstan to bring natural gas into Russia to supplement domestic consumption. The Nord Stream natural gas pipeline scheduled for completion in 2010 will link Russia directly to the German market across the Baltic Sea. China has also become a more aggressive player in regional energy markets, and a major pipeline linking Kazakhstan to China's Xinjiang region is currently under construction. In some ways, the only major loser in the pipeline wars of the Caspian has been Iran, which has been effectively isolated, deprived of investment, and excluded from major pipeline routes.

The "great game" for access to Caspian resources has led to a healthy diversification of export arteries for which there is an objective need. It has helped the new independent states of the region find traction in their dealings with the great powers who have become rivals for regional influence. The rivalry is still underway nonetheless. In the Caspian region, in the words of Régis Genté, oil and natural gas "also represent the means by which a struggle to control the center of the Eurasian continent is waged."[29] But the new great game has been driven by geostrategic considerations that have often warred against economic logic—the exclusion of southern routings transiting Iran is a good example—and encouraged zero-sum gambits that have hindered the cause of rational exploitation and distribution. Moreover, the flood of oil revenues into the fragile polities of the region has given an impetus to corruption and reinforced authoritarian governance.

The United States has been successful in achieving some of its basic policy goals in the region. Building on the BTC and in cooperation with European partners, it is in the process of creating an east-west transit corridor that will bind the Caspian region more closely to the West.[30] It has broken Russia's monopoly of access. It has created space for states like Georgia and Azerbaijan to lessen their dependence on their great neighbor to the north and pursue more autonomous national policies. These successes have created friction with Russia, Iran, and China on other fronts. Russia, in particular, will remain an indispensable source of hydrocarbon resources, particularly on the European market, no matter how much supply may be supplemented by drawing on Caspian reserves.[31] Iran's energy potential remains a wild card that could impact significantly upon world markets. In the longer term, global energy security will need to be pursued by cooperative polices uniting producers and consumers in a search for sustainable equilibrium of supply and demand. On this level, the competitive great game of the post-Soviet Caspian does not offer a positive example, and the issue of long-term energy security in Eurasia remains open.

The Global War on Terrorism.

The southern tier of the Eurasian land mass, approximately contiguous with what Zbigniew Brzezinski has trenchantly described as an "arc of crisis" or "whirlpool of violence" co-terminus with the great crescent of Islamic civilization, is a zone of mobilization for the world's most threatening and aggressively anti-American jihadist terrorist groupings, including the remnants of Osama Bin Laden's original al-Qaeda organization.[32] It is the primary arena within which what may still be referred to as the global war on terrorism must be waged and won. Inner Asia is an essential operating base for this effort. The geographical belt paralleling the southern flank of the Russian Federation, rich in strategic resources and geopolitical potential, also has inherent strategic significance and has become a bone of contention between aspiring regional and global powers. It is one of the most conflict prone regions in world politics, and the most important market for global arms transfers, currently absorbing over half the world total.

The Islamic factor is a constant throughout the region, but it is difficult to generalize about its effects. Most area states are fragile post-communist polities or developing nations that threaten to be overwhelmed by flawed transitions and frustrated modernization. Islamic radicalism is one of the directions into which accumulating political and socio-economic frustrations are being channeled.[33]

Promoting regional stability in the larger sense, including commitments to democratization, social equity, and good governance, remains the foundation of U.S. regional policy. A significant part of the threat of transnational terrorism in the area grows out of the activities of criminal networks, illegal trafficking, and widespread corruption that only a long-term development strategy can address. This should not in any way be construed as a war against Islam. From the Balkans into Inner Asia, the Islamic factor can become a force working for social cohesion and development if it is embraced and absorbed into an emerging modern civic culture that accepts the premises of tolerance, openness, and respect for diversity. But the imminent threat of jihadist violence must also be addressed. Moreover, unresolved or latent conflicts such as those in Kosovo, Iraq, Kurdistan, Nagorno-Karabakh, Chechnya, and the northern Caucasus, Georgia, Afghanistan and Pakistan, and Kashmir all involve an Islamic dimension.

From a U.S. perspective, the ongoing struggle against the Taliban and their legacy in Afghanistan and Pakistan will remain a priority for some time.[34] Promoting the nation-building process in Afghanistan and balancing the need for stability and modernization in Pakistan are long-term undertakings that will require a consistent application of military, diplomatic, cultural, and economic resources. Efforts to open access to the region by developing an east-west transportation corridor parallel to the EU's TRACECA project bypassing Russia to the south is also threatened by instability derived from Eurasia's so-called "frozen conflicts" and transnational terrorist access to the region.[35] Political initiatives designed to facilitate negotiated solutions to the issues of Kosovo, Transnistria, Abkhazia and South Ossetia, and Nagorno-Karabakh are important components of regional strategy. Cultivation of positive relations, expanded security cooperation with a variety of regional states, and strategic access including possible basing and over-flight rights are likewise significant. This may include promoting the eventual association of Eurasian partners with key European and transatlantic organizations. Security cooperation efforts include a focus on building partner capability to secure critical infrastructure, lines of communication, and strategic resources on their own national territory as well as globally. In southeastern Europe, the development of Joint Task Force East locations in Romania and Bulgaria, and in the southern Caucasus the cultivation of Azerbaijan and Georgia as potential access nations can help facilitate U.S. strategic reach. Security cooperation also demands the promotion of defense and security sector reform aimed at the development of modern, professional military and security systems subordinated to stable, democratically-empowered civilian leadership.

An intrusive security posture in Inner Asia associated with the pursuit of the global war on terrorism has created friction in U.S. relations with Russia and China. Concern over U.S. intentions has encouraged wider collaboration between Moscow and Beijing, most visibly manifested by the development of the Shanghai Cooperation Organization (SCO).[36] From its origin the SCO has issued more or less overt criticisms of U.S. security policy and practice in Inner Asia, and a July 2005 leadership statement called upon the U.S.-led coalition engaged in antiterrorist activities in Afghanistan to provide a timetable for the withdrawal of its bases in Central Asia.[37] Chinese analysts argue that the U.S. emphasis upon antiterrorism is linked with a geostrategic agenda seeking to dominate the region and use it as a source of leverage against great power rivals.[38] Russia opportunistically exploited Uzbek concern over U.S. reactions to the Andijon incident of May 2005 to achieve the closure of the U.S. air base at Karshi Khanabad.[39]

In the case of Russia, such friction derives in part from a more comprehensive disintegration of its bilateral relationship with Washington, with multiple causes. It does not necessarily reflect fundamental disagreements about the nature of the war against terrorism or the pursuit of security interests in Inner Asia. Russia, perhaps more than any country in the world, is closely aligned with the U.S. definition of the terrorist threat. It understands the complex security challenges associated with the phenomenon of Islamism, including ways in which mal-governance and criminalization impact upon the long-term goal of promoting stability in the Islamic world.[40] Russia confronts a major threat of jihadist terrorism in areas adjacent to and within its borders which it is in the U.S.

interest to help it contain.[41] U.S. goals in Afghanistan and Pakistan are not antithetical to its purpose.[42]

This coincidence of purpose applies to a wider spectrum of security interests. Nonproliferation, countering criminal trafficking, the campaign against religious extremism and transnational terrorism, limiting conventional arms racing, and addressing ecological disasters all represent substantial mutual concerns. In the words of one regional analyst, "Washington and Moscow . . . have a real opportunity for coordinating their Central Asian policies on the basis of their common strategic interests."[43] Strategic competition with both Russia and China in Inner Asia is inevitable, but it can be combined with prudent cooperation in areas of shared interest.

Regional Order.

Forward positioning in Europe under the aegis of the NATO alliance remains the *sine qua non* of a successful U.S.-Eurasian policy. Alliance maintenance, cooperation with traditional European allies, and an awareness of the continued vitality of the Alliance itself as a basis for a dynamic U.S. world role are the foundations for success. NATO, notably through the Partnership for Peace program, continues to play a positive role as a force for transition in the security sector and source of inclusion throughout Eurasia. The NATO-Russia Council provides an important institutional link to Moscow. NATO deployments in Afghanistan are making a useful, albeit limited, contribution to the global war on terrorism. As the Alliance continues its evolution from the collective defense forum of the Cold War decades to a more broadly based collective security community, its role in

Eurasia will increase. The United States should support and encourage this evolution. Sustained association with traditional European allies is a vital U.S. interest. Europe remains an indispensable platform for U.S. global engagement.[44]

U.S. initiative may become even more important in view of the EU's manifest inability to develop a dynamic and engaging Eurasian policy. EU relations with the Russian Federation are troubled, and the promise of "strategic partnership" a fading dream.[45] The new EU member states that have emerged from the ranks of Soviet Socialist Republics or the Warsaw Pact have proven to be a significant lobby for policies blocking extensive cooperation with Moscow. Key European states have reacted badly to human rights abuses and the perceived unreliability of Russian energy supply. The EU's European Neighbourhood Policy (ENP), designed to create a "common space" in the central European corridor between Russia and the EU proper, has generated considerable resentment in Moscow, where it is perceived as yet another form of encroachment on Russia's legitimate sphere of influence.[46] The ENP has also closed the door to realistic prospects for membership on the part of western leaning polities such as Georgia and Ukraine.[47] In some measure, these failures are due to the EU's inability to overcome its chronic deficiencies as a strategic actor.

NATO's role in the new Eurasia will be limited by the need to sustain cooperative relations with the Russian Federation. Influential members of the Russian armed forces and national security community cling to an image of NATO and the United States as traditional security threats. Militarily, Moscow will continue to view Eurasia as a sphere of special interest where Western influence should be limited to the extent possible, and it can bring powerful policy instruments to bear in pursuit of its goals. Most of the new independent states of post-Soviet Eurasia depend heavily upon Russia in one way or another—accumulated debt, energy dependency, security guarantees, labor migration and remissions, and political support all provide meaningful sources of leverage.[48] Of course, subservience to Moscow's direction can be challenged. The "colored revolutions" in Georgia and Ukraine (and to a lesser extent Kyrgyzstan) illustrate various kinds of defiance to heavy-handed direction from Moscow, albeit with mixed outcomes.[49] Georgia remains an outspoken opponent of Russian prerogatives and close U.S. ally and has demonstrated the will to stand up to Russian pressure.[50] But the ambiguous results of the "Orange Revolution" in Ukraine sound a note of caution concerning what can be expected from this kind of political initiative in cases were public opinion is divided and links to Russia remains strong.[51] Russia has consistently denounced the phenomenon of "colored revolutions" as a strategy of destabilization promoted from abroad, and is actively and openly promoting a reversal of their consequences.[52]

Russia's relations with its Eurasian neighbors are conducted on a traditional bilateral basis as well as in the context of a growing number of forums for multilateral association. This represents an effort to organize the Eurasian space in political and economic terms distinct from a European project from which Russia has been excluded. It also means creating some kind of strategic balance against NATO and the United States. The cautious and pragmatic initiatives of the NATO-Russia Council are not sufficiently robust to offset concern for Western military penetration. The legacy of NATO's war in Kosovo, repositioning of U.S. forces into the wider Black Sea area, the ongoing dynamic of NATO enlargement, U.S. and NATO refusal to ratify an amended version of the Conventional Forces in Europe Treaty pending a Russian pull-out from Moldova and Georgia, long-term basing arrangements in Inner Asia, and U.S. plans to construct missile defense systems in central Europe have all created concern. Indeed, Russian Chief of Staff Iurii Baluevskii has pointed to the U.S. commitment to "expanding its economic, political, and military presence in Russia's traditional zones of influence" as his country's top national security threat.[53]

The CIS clings to a kind of half-life, useful as a forum for certain kinds of interaction and association but painfully short of dynamism. Russian sources continue to cite its relevance, particularly as a forum for economic coordination.[54] At the CIS summit in 2003, four countries—Russia, Ukraine, Kazakhstan, and Belarus—signed an agreement establishing a unified economic space with the goals of eliminating tariffs and harmonizing markets in key areas such as transport and energy. The Eurasian Economic Community, which emerged from the CIS Customs Union in 2001, is a useful vehicle for harmonizing exchange. Its association with the Central Asian Cooperation Organization (Kazakhstan, Kyrgyzstan, Tajikistan, and Uzbekistan) makes it a broader Eurasian forum. The Collective Security Treaty Organization (CSTO) also emerged from within the CIS.[55] Since 2002 it has striven to assert its legitimacy as a regional collective security forum, and Russian Defense Minister Sergei Ivanov has spoken of the CSTO as a potential Eurasian partner for NATO.[56] The most substantial of the new Eurasian forums is the SCO. It has undertaken significant initiatives, particularly in coordinating antiterror activities, but it is also a forum within which Russia will be condemned to play second fiddle to its dynamic Chinese partner.

The United States has actively resisted Russian efforts to use the CIS as a vehicle for encouraging reconsolidation of the post-Soviet space. Since 1996 it has supported the activities of the GUUAM forum (an association of Georgia, Ukraine, Uzbekistan, Azerbaijan, and Moldova) as a means of resisting Russian influence. In May 2006, following Uzbekistan's withdrawal, a rechristened Organization for Democracy and Development-GUAM, picked up the torch.[57] Some analysts have argued that the United States would benefit from establishing more formal ties with Eurasia's Russian-sponsored economic and security forums, but to date without success.[58] None of these new Eurasian multilateral forums is particularly strong for the time being—they can still safely be neglected or ignored. In the longer term, however, a refusal to develop more formal ties may become counterproductive. While none of these organizations is so robust as to pose a meaningful threat to U.S. interests, they do have the potential to contribute to the overarching goal of regional stability. The United States should avoid turning support for GUAM into a zero-sum game with Russia for influence in a region where both parties have important interests at stake. The organization should be crafted to complement, rather than compete with the CIS, by encouraging overlapping association and cooperative programs. The United States should likewise avoid the trap of pursuing an assertive containment policy toward Russia in areas where powerful interdependencies militate against its success.[59]

Russia is also a member of the Organization of the Black Sea Economic Cooperation (within which the United States maintains observer status) and is actively engaged in what U.S. strategists have taken to calling the wider Black Sea area. This complex region is perceived as an emerging area of economic opportunity, an integral part of a viable Europe-Caucasus-Asia transport corridor, and a potential strategic buttress against threats emerging from the Islamic Middle East. Some analysts have called for a Black Sea strategy specifically designed to exclude Russian influence.[60] This kind of approach risks provoking competitive reactions and countervailing associations that will make it more difficult to achieve foreign policy goals.[61] A better approach would build on policies of inclusion and broad based cooperation. Of particular importance are efforts already underway to rescue the U.S.-Turkish strategic relationship from the pressures to which it has been subjected during the war in Iraq.[62]

Relations with the Russian Federation.

U.S. policy toward the Russian Federation asserts an aspiration to partnership and a commitment to pragmatic cooperation in areas of common interest.[63] This is combined with a more aggressive commitment to "push back on negative Russian behavior."[64] In practice, throughout the 1990s a weakened Moscow had little choice but to bow, albeit often begrudgingly, to U.S. initiatives when national priorities diverged. To a certain extent, Washington may have become accustomed to Russian compliance. Today's Russian Federation is a much more dynamic and ambitious polity with a stronger sense of its prerogatives. Putin's Russia has repeatedly asserted its determination to pursue autonomous national policies irrespective of the opinions of others.⁶⁵ Its responses to policy disagreements with the United States have become uncooperative and obstructive.⁶⁶ The parallel pursuit of the goals of encouraging Russia's development as a "stable geopolitical partner" and "pushing back" against perceived misbehavior may no longer be a productive course of action on either count.

The state of Russian-American relations has become affected by rhetorical excess on both sides, perhaps culminating with Putin's remarks to the 2007 Munich *Wehrkunde* publicly condemning a "unipolar" model of world order where "one state, the United States, has overstepped its national borders in every sphere."⁶⁷ Much of the rhetoric has been aimed at domestic constituencies, but the impact of such vituperative language should not be underestimated. It fairly reflects a troubled relationship where cooperative initiatives are losing ground. In the United States, there is bipartisan concern over Russia's less cooperative domestic and international agendas. A recent report by the Council on Foreign Relations under the general direction of Senators John Edwards and Jack Kemp is sharply critical of Russia's "wrong direction" and recommends a retreat from a commitment to "broad partnership" to a more discrete policy of "selective cooperation."⁶⁸ Expressions of dissent from this near consensus sound like voices in the wilderness.⁶⁹ In Russia, the dominant tone of the state-influenced Russian media, academic commentary, and official discourse is highly critical of the United States.⁷⁰ If policy discourse is any measure, the current state of Russian-American relations is grim and shows no signs of immediate improvement.

Russia is nonetheless a potentially vital partner for the successful pursuit of U.S. interests in the new Eurasia. The viability of the nonproliferation regime, international pressure to break the dynamic of proliferation in the cases of North Korea and Iran, counterterrorism efforts and the defeat of jihadist offensives, energy and environmental security, nuclear strategic stability, movement toward a viable Eurasian regional order including deepening democratization and an enlarged and stable Euro-Atlantic community, and cooperative security initiatives among the great powers of East Asia (China, Japan, South Korea, Russia, and the United States) all depend upon working with, rather than against, the Russian Federation. The gravitational pull of a reviving Russian Federation as a force in Eurasia, based on its central role in existing energy systems and transportation infrastructure, profound economic dependencies, extensive capital investment, importance as a market and destination for labor migration, primacy in regional security structures, and cultural strength is incontrovertible. This is a Russia whose intent should be understood as to "reinvigorate the former Soviet space, not as a historical atavism in the Soviet mold but as a developing economic zone with Russia as its powerful center."[71]

Cooperation with the Russian Federation need not be a pipe dream. Programs already in place, such as the Cooperative Threat Reduction initiative, designed to help Russia cope with the threat of proliferation, or security cooperation initiatives on a military-to-military level, function rather well. Despite the relative progress that it has recently enjoyed, Russia also needs positive and productive relations with the United States and the West to further the process of modernization, facilitate integration with the world economy, tap Western technological potential to exploit its own immense resources fully, and to accomplish basic national security goals in the Eurasian area.[72]

Henry Kissinger has sagely remarked of the U.S.-Russian relationship that "differences among states are inevitable when their interests diverge. But these differences can be mitigated, for they are not, in fact, all that great, when they are placed alongside a larger sphere of cooperation."[73] Finding ways to expand this sphere of cooperation is an important and difficult challenge for a successful U.S. Eurasian policy.

Summary and Conclusion.

The key issues that define U.S. interests in the new Eurasia are energy security, counterterrorism and Islamism, counterproliferation, and great power rivalry. These interests are transnational and transregional in character.

- Defined as the dual continents of Europe and Asia, the new Eurasia includes a critical mass of world energy reserves. Ensuring access by cultivating relations with producer states, constructing and maintaining reliable pipeline infrastructure, guaranteeing strategic lines of communication, and defending political stability in conflict prone regions are vital to the United States and its allies. They are also important prerequisites for the balanced development for regional states.

- Eurasia encompasses most of the most important centers of contemporary Islamic civilization. It has been the cradle for many of the most militant anti-U.S. jihadist movements. The Eurasian arena will be an important crucible for relations between Islam and the West for decades. The United States needs to prevail in Afghanistan and address the threat of Islamic terrorism in the short term while simultaneously pursuing a policy of dialogue and inclusion designed to prevent the emergence of a "clash of civilizations" with the potential to open a confessional divide.

- The new Eurasia has also become an area of strategic interaction between great powers, including the EU, United States, Russia, China, and India. The new "Great Game" in Inner Asia is not just a clever phrase—it references the reality of increasingly sharp geopolitical competition for leverage and influence. The United States will resist the emergence of a single hegemonic power in the Eurasian heartland. It should also be wary of the development of countervailing coalitions (such as the SCO might become under certain circumstances) that draw on anti-Americanism as a source of cohesion. Washington must pursue its interests in economic and strategic access, democratic transformation, and regional stability. But relations between the great powers in Eurasia need not inevitably lead to conflict. There are significant mutual interests at play (including the common goal of resisting proliferation and reinforcing strategic stability) as well as areas of discord.

- Russia has the potential to make important contributions to the successful pursuit of U.S. interests in the new Eurasia. Managing the U.S.-Russian relationship so as to make the pragmatic pursuit of mutually beneficial policies possible is an important challenge.

The new Eurasia is a wide stage upon which many of the most critical issues confronting the United States and its allies will be worked out in the decades to come. In order to define and pursue U.S. interests effectively, it is important to develop policies that conceptualize and address them in an appropriately broad context.

ENDNOTES - U.S. INTERESTS IN NEW EURASIA

1. In Mackinder's famous dictum, "Who rules the Heartland commands the World-Island; Who rules the World-Island commands the World." Halford Mackinder, *Democratic Ideals and Reality,* New York: W. W. Norton & Company, 1962, p. xviii.

2. P. Struve, "Istoricheskaia sushchnost' Russkoi revoliutsii i natsional'nye tseli" ("The Historical Essence of the Russian Revolution and National Goals"), *Ocherki o russkoi revoliutsii,* Moscow, 1990, pp. 247-248.

3. Nicholas Berdiaev, *The Russian Idea,* Boston: Beacon Press, 1962, p. 2.

4. Jean-Marie Duroselle, *Tout Empire périra: Théorie des relations internationales* (*All Empires Perish: The Theory of International Relations*), Paris, 1992, pp. 284-310.

5. V. V. Sogrin, "1985-1995: Realii i utopii novoi Rossii" ("1985-1995: Realities and Utopias of the New Russia"), *Otechestvennaia istoriia,* No. 2, 1995, pp. 9-10.

6. Anders Åslund, "Russia's Success Story," *Foreign Affairs,* September/October 1994, pp. 58-71.

7. The first citation is from Richard Pipes, *Russian Conservatism and its Critics: A Study in Russian Political Culture,* New Haven: Yale University Press, 2005, p. 1; and the second from Adam Ulam, *Expansion and Coexistence: Soviet Foreign Policy 1917-73,* 2nd ed., New York: Holt, Rinehart and Winston, Inc. 1974, p. 377.

8. Richard Pipes, "Russia's Choice," *Commentary,* March 1992, pp. 28-33.

9. Zbigniew Brzezinski, "A Plan for Europe," *Foreign Affairs,* January/February 1995, p. 31.

10. "Kuda idet Rossiia? 10 let reforma. Zasedanie 'Kruglogo stola'" ("Wither Russia? 10 Years of Reform. A Round Table

Session"), *Otechestevennaia istoriia*, No. 4, 1995, p. 198. Alekandr Solzhenitsyn, *Rossiia v Obvale* (*Russia in Ruins*), Moscow: Russkii put', 1998, states this perception powerfully.

11. See Andrei P. Tsyganov, *Russia's Foreign Policy: Change and Continuity in National Identity*, Lanham, MD: Rowan & Littlefield Publishers, Inc., 2006, pp. 78-81.

12. Sergei Rogov, *Evraziiskaia strategiia dlia Rossii* (*A Eurasian Strategy for Russia*), Moscow: Institute SShA i Kanady, 1998.

13. *Obzor vneshnei politiki Rossiiskoi Federatsii* (*Survey of the Foreign Policy of the Russian Federation*), Moscow: Foreign Ministry of the Russian Federation, 2007, p. 28.

14. Sergei Markov speaking to the conference "The EU and Russia: Challenges of a Pan-European Perspective," Forlì, Italy, April 29, 2007.

15. Dmitry Shapentokh, "Dugin, Eurasianism, and Central Asia," *Communist and Post-Communist Studies*, Vol. 40, No. 2, June 2007, pp. 143-156; and Jacob W. Kipp, "Aleksandr Dugin and the Ideology of National Revival: Geopolitics, Eurasianism and the Conservative Revolution," *European Security*, Vol. 11, No. 3, Autumn 2003, pp. 91-125.

16. This is a major theme of Aleksandr Dugin, *Misterii Evrazii* (*Mysteries of Eurasia*), Moscow: Arktogeia, 1998, sometimes described as the "manifesto" of the contemporary Russian Eurasian school.

17. U.S. Department of State/USAID, *Joint Strategic Plan, 2007-2012*, Washington, DC: U.S. Department of State, 2007.

18. See Tim McDaniel, *The Agony of the Russian Idea*, Princeton: Princeton University Press, 1996; and Dmitri Trenin, *The End of Eurasia: Russia on the Border between Geopolitics and Globalization*, Washington, DC: Carnegie Endowment for International Peace, 2002.

19. In his seminal work, Mackinder defines the heartland quite expansively. "The Heartland, for the purposes of strategical thinking, includes the Baltic Sea, the navigable Middle and Lower Danube, the Black Sea, Asia Minor, Armenia, Persia, Tibet, and Mongolia. Within it, therefore, were Brandenburg-Prussia and Austria-Hungary, as well as Russia—a vast triple base of manpower." Mackinder, *Democratic Ideals and Reality*, New York: Henry Holt and Company, 1919, p. 72. The concept of the world

island is defined even more expansively as "the joint continent of Europe, Asia, and Africa." *Ibid.*, p. 45.

20. Cynthia A. Roberts, *Russia and the European Union: The Sources and Limits of "Special Relationships,"* Carlisle, PA: U.S. Army War College, Strategic Studies Institute, February 2007, p. 49.

21. Christophe-Alexandre Paillard, "Gazprom: Mode d'emploi pour un suicide énergétique" ("Gazprom: How to Commit Energy Suicide"), *Russie. NEI, Visions,* No. 17, IFRI, March 2007.

22. Aleksandr Gabuev, "Kholodnana voina prishla na sever," ("The Cold War Comes to the North"), *Kommersant,* August 4, 2007.

23. See Steve Levine, *The Oil and the Glory: The Pursuit of Empire and Fortune on the Caspian Sea,* New York: Random House, 2007.

24. Cited from *www.state.gov/www/regions/nis/970721talbott.html*.

25. *BP Statistical Review of World Energy,* London: British Petroleum, 2006. Iran's portion of the seabed remains partially unexplored.

26. Gawdat Bahgat, "Prospects for Energy Cooperation in the Caspian Sea," *Communist and Post-Communist Studies,* Vol. 40. No. 2, June 2007, pp. 157-168.

27. *Ibid.*, p. 166.

28. Ilan Greenberg and Andrew E. Kramer, "Cheney Urges Kazakhs to Bypass Russia," *International Herald Tribune,* May 6, 2006.

29. Régis Genté, "Du Caucase à l'Asie centrale, 'grand jeu' autour du pétrole et du gaz" ("From the Caucasus of Central Asia, 'Great Game' Around Fuel and Gas"), *Le Monde diplomatique,* June 2007, p. 18.

30. Brenda Schaffer, "From Pipedream to Pipeline: A Caspian Success Story," *Current History,* Vol. 104, No. 684, October 2005, p. 243.

31. P. Kanygin, "Energeticheskaia bezopasnost' Evropy i interesy Rossii," ("The Energy Security of Europe and the Interests of Russia"), *Mirovaia ekonomika i mezhdunarodnye otnosheniia,* No. 5, 2007, pp. 3-11.

32. Zbigniew Brzezinski, *Out of Control: Global Turmoil on the Eve of the Twentieth Century,* New York: Collier Books, 1993, p. 163.

33. See Ahmed Rashid, *Jihad: The Rise of Militant Islam in Central Asia*, New Haven: Yale University Press, 2003.

34. Thomas H. Johnson and M. Chris Mason, "Understanding the Taliban and Insurgency in Afghanistan," *Orbis*, Winter 2007, pp. 71-89.

35. For background, see Dov Lynch, *Engaging Eurasia's Separatist States: Unresolved Conflicts and de facto States*, Washington, DC: U.S. Institute of Peace, 2004.

36. Launched in 1996 as the Shanghai Five and renamed the Shanghai Cooperation Organization in 2001, the organization includes China, Russia, Kazakhstan, Kyrgyzstan, Tajikistan, and Uzbekistan as full members; and Iran, Pakistan, India, and Mongolia as observers.

37. "Declaration of Heads of Member States of Shanghai Cooperation Organization," Astana, July 5, 2005, at *www.sectsco.org*.

38. Chzhao Khuashen, *Kitai, tsentral'naia aziia i shankhaiskaia organizatsiia sotrudnichestva* (*China, Central Asia, and the Shanghai Cooperation Organization*), Working Paper No. 5, Moscow: Carnegie Moscow Center, 2005, pp. 41-44; and Bates Gill, *Rising Star: China's New Security Diplomacy*, Washington, DC: Brookings Institution Press, 2007, pp. 149-151.

39. Eugene Rumer, "The U.S. Interests and Role in Central Asia after K2," *The Washington Quarterly*, Vol. 29, No. 3, Summer 2006, pp. 141-154. The U.S. Government had criticized the Uzbek government's use of excessive force to repress rioting in the city of Andijon in May 2005.

40. Svante E. Cornell and Niklas L. P. Swanstrom, "The Eurasian Drug Trade: A Challenge to Regional Security," *Problems of Post-Communism*, Vol. 53, No. 4, July/August 2006, pp. 10-28.

41. Gordon M. Hahn, *Russia's Islamic Threat*, New Haven: Yale University Press, 2007, pp. 234-240.

42. In a Joint Declaration of March 26, 2007, Russia and China state that:

> Russia and China favor continuing efforts for the peaceful reconstruction of Afghanistan, and support the positive efforts of the government of Afghanistan on behalf of socio-economic development, post-war reconstruction, the development of good neighborly

relations and friendship, and the rapid transformation of Afghanistan into a peaceful, secure, and economically prosperous government.

These are identical to U.S. goals. "Sovmestnaia deklaratsiia Rossiiskoi Federatsii i Kitaiskoi Narodnoi Respubliki," ("Joint Declaration of the Russian Federation and the People's Republic of China"), *Problemy Dal'nego Vostoka,* No. 3, 2007, p. 11.

43. Farkhod Tolipov, "The Strategic Dilemma of Central Asia," *Russia in Global Affairs,* No. 4, October-December 2006, p. 22.

44. The U.S. State Department's current Joint Strategic Plan describes Europe, "including NATO, OSCE, the Organization for Economic Cooperation and Development, and the EU agenda," as "a platform for global transformational diplomacy." *Joint Strategic Plan 2007-2012.*

45. Maurizio Massari, "Russia and the EU Ten Years On: A Relationship in Search of Definition," *The International Spectator,* Vol. 42, No. 1, March 2007, pp. 1-15.

46. N. Arbatova, "Obshchee politicheskoe prostranstvo mezhdu Rossiei i ES: Utopiia ili real'nost'? ("A Common Political Space between Russia and the EU: Utopia or Reality?"), *Mirovaia ekonomika i mezhdunarodnye otnosheniia,* No. 12, 2006, pp. 3-12.

47. Karen E. Smith, "The Outsiders: The European Neighbourhood Policy," *International Affairs,* Vol. 81, No. 4, 2005, pp. 757-773.

48. Fiona Hill, "Moscow Discovers Soft Power," *Current History,* Vol. 105, No. 693, October 2006, pp. 341-347.

49. For mature evaluations of these events, see Graeme P. Herd, "Colorful Revolutions and the CIS: 'Manufactured' Versus 'Managed' Democracy," *Problems of Post-Communism,* Vol. 52, No. 2, March/April 2005, pp. 3-18; Tom Wood, "Reflections on the Revolution in Kyrgyzstan," *The Fletcher Forum of World Affairs,* Vol. 30, No. 2, Summer 2006, pp. 43-56; Vladimir Papava, "The Political Economy of Georgia's Rose Revolution," *Orbis,* Vol. 50, No. 4, Fall 2006, pp. 657-667.

50. Anatolii Gordienko, "Saakashvili zagovoril o Rossii v tret'em litse," ("Saakashvili Spoke of Russia in the Third Person"), *Nezavisimaia gazeta,* December 29, 2006. Georgia is a major contributor to Operation IRAQI FREEDOM and Kosovo Forces (KFOR).

51. Ianina Sokolovskaia, "Zhdat' li Ukraina novoi revoliutsii?" ("Does Ukrania Confront a New Revolution?"), *Izvestiia*, July 6, 2006.

52. V. S. Kotliar, "Mezhdunarodnoe pravo i fenomen 'tsvetnykh revoliutsii' v stranakh SNG," ("International Law and the Phenomenon of 'Colored Revolutions' in the Countries of the CIS"), *Gosudarstvo i pravo*, No. 5, 2007, pp. 71-76.

53. Vladimir Isachenkov, "Baluyevsky Calls U.S. Expansion a Threat," *The Moscow Times*, February 12, 2007, p. 4.

54. N. Shumskii, "Strategiia razvitiia Sodruzhestva Nezavisimykh Gosudarstv,"("The Development Strategy of the Commonwealth of Independent States"), *Voprosy ekonomiki*, No. 12, 2006, pp. 128-138; and N. Fedulova, "Sodruzhestvo Nezavisimykh Gosudarstv—15 let spustia," ("The Commonwealth of Independent States—15 Years Later"), *Mirovaia ekonomika i mezhdunarodnye otnosheniia*, No. 12, 2006, pp. 82-91.

55. Adam Weinstein, "Russian Phoenix: The Collective Security Treaty Organization," *The Whitehead Journal of Diplomacy*, Vol. VIII, No. 1, Winter/Spring 2007, pp. 167-180.

56. According to Ivanov, "the next logical step may be to work out a mechanism for cooperation between NATO and the CSTO with corresponding, clearly defined spheres of responsibility." Cited in Vladimir Mukhin, "Novyi razdel Evrasii," ("A New Partition of Eurasia"), *Nezavismaia gazeta*, December 4, 2006. CSTO members are Russia, Armenia, Belarus, Kazakhstan, Kyrgyzstan, and Tajikistan. Russia's clear preeminence within the organization limits its legitimacy.

57. Anna Iaz'kova, "Ekspansiia svobody na postsovetskom prostranstve" ("The Expansion of Freedom within the Post-Soviet Space"), *Nezavisimaia gazeta*, June 5, 2006.

58. Richard Weitz, "Averting a New Great Game in Central Asia," *The Washington Quarterly*, Vol. 29, No. 3, Summer 2006, pp. 163-164.

59. Yuliya Timoshenko, "Containing Russia," *Foreign Affairs*, Vol. 86, No. 3, May/June 2007, pp. 69-82.

60. Bruce P. Jackson, "The 'Soft War' for Europe's East," *Policy Review*, No. 137, June/July 2006, pp. 3-14.

61. Fiona Hill and Omer Taspinar, "Turkey and Russia: Axis of the Excluded," *Survival*, Vol. 48, No. 1, Spring 2006, pp. 81-92.

62. Aylin Güney, "An Anatomy of the Transformation of the U.S.-Turkish Alliance: From 'Cold War' to 'War on Iraq'," *Turkish Studies*, Vol. 6, No. 3, September 2005, pp. 341-359; and Michael M. Gunter, "The U.S.-Turkish Alliance in Disarray," *World Affairs*, Vol. 167, No. 3, Winter 2005, pp. 113-123.

63. See the remarks made at the Embassy of the Russian Federation by Under Secretary of State for Political Affairs R. Nicholas Burns in "Commemorating the 200th Anniversary of U.S.-Russia Relations," January 30, 2007, at *www.state.gov/p/us/rm/2007/80198.htm*. Burns asserts that "we have a partnership with Russia."

64. Examples of negative Russian behavior are elaborated in the Department of State/USAID, *Joint Strategic Plan 2007-2012*:

> Increasing centralization of power, pressure on NGOs and civil society, a growing government role in the economy, and restrictions on media freedom have all emerged as clear and worrisome trends. Russian weapon sales to such states as Iran, Syria, and Venezuela are also cause for great concern throughout the international community. Russia's policy toward its neighbors is another major challenge, especially Moscow's support for separatist regions in Georgia and Moldova, its political and economic pressure against Georgia, and its monopolistic use of energy to pressure neighboring states and gain control of infrastructure and strategic assets.

65. "Vneshnepoliticheskaia samostoiatel'nost' Rossii—bezuslovnyi imperativ" ("Russia's Foreign Policy Independence—An Unconditional Imperative"), *Moskovskie Novosti*, July 11, 2007.

66. In remarks to the U.S. Senate Foreign Relations Committee, Assistant Secretary of State Daniel Fried noted that:

> In the past few months, Russian leaders and senior officials have, in quick succession: threatened to suspend Russia's obligations under the Treaty on Conventional Armed Forces in Europe, the CFE Treaty; criticized U.S. plans for a modest missile defense system based in Europe and rejected our explanation that it is intended to counter potential threats from Iran, only to propose missile defense cooperation in Azerbaijan; attacked U.S.

agreements with Romania and Bulgaria to establish joint training facilities in those countries, even though this would involve no permanent stationing of U.S. forces; left the impression that there's no will to find a realistic, prompt resolution of Kosovo's final status; threatened the territorial integrity of Georgia and Moldova by giving renewed support to separatist regimes and issuing veiled threats to recognize breakaway regions in those countries; further restricted freedom of assembly and association by preventing peaceful demonstrations as well as hindering the operation of organizations such as Internews.

"Russia and U.S.-Russia Relations," Remarks before the U.S. Senate Foreign Relations Committee, Daniel Fried, Assistant Secretary of State for European and Eurasian Affairs, June 21, 2007, at *www.state.gov/p/eur/rls/rm/86990.htm*.

67. "Vystuplenie prezidenta Rossii Vladimira Putina na Miunkhenskoi konferentsii po voprosam politiki bezopasnosti 10 Fevralia 2007 goda," ("Address of Russian President Vladimir Putin to the Munich Conference on Security Policy, February 10, 2007"), *Izvestiia*, February 13, 2007.

68. *Russia's Wrong Direction: What the United States Can and Should Do*, Council on Foreign Relations Independent Task Force Report No. 57, New York: Council on Foreign Relations, 2006.

69. One example is Gary Hart, "Don't Lose Russia: Letter to Democrats," *The National Interest*, No. 88, March/April 2007, pp. 23-25.

70. Anatolii Utkin, *Amerikanskaia imperiia* (*The American Empire*), Moscow: Izdatel'stvo Eksmo, 2003, provides a substantial example of this kind of analysis.

71. Roberts, *Russia and the European Union*, p. 62.

72. Dmitrii Trenin, "Pochemu Amerika i Rossiia nuzhny drug drugu" ("Why Russia and America Need One Another"), *Pro et Contra*, No. 2, Issue 36, March-April 2007, pp. 6-17.

73. Cited in Artur Blinov, "Genri Kissindzher: Moskva i Vashington dolzhny sotrudnichat'" ("Henry Kissinger: Moscow and Washington Must Cooperate"), *Nezavisimaia gazeta*, June 7, 2006.

RUSSIA'S THREAT PERCEPTION AND STRATEGIC POSTURE

Dmitri Trenin

Between 2003 and 2005, Russia finally decoupled from the West in terms of its foreign policy orientation. Russia is now on its own, unashamedly pursuing its self-interest. Moscow's estrangement from the United States and the European Union (EU) has major implications for Russian security and defense policy. This paper will discuss Russia's threat perception and its strategic posture.

Strategic Philosophy.

Russian strategic policymakers have no ideology. However, they respect what they regard as the laws of *Realpolitik*. They believe that all nations seek to expand their influence, and in order to do so they rely on their power, both hard and soft. In their view, military force is a usable tool of foreign policy, and war can be a legitimate extension of policy: war prevention is not enough. They focus on states' military capabilities, rather than their political affiliations. Essentially this means that any country with a substantial military potential—whether an advanced Western democracy, an emerging Asian power, or a restive Middle Eastern regime—can become a threat to Russia under the circumstances. This highly pessimistic worldview, which results from the analysis of post-Cold War strategic developments, represents a near-total repudiation of the Mikhail Gorbachev and early Boris Yeltsin-era philosophy of common security.

Demilitarization of Russian strategic thinking is a thing of the past. This, however, does not mean a return to the Cold War mentality. More likely, Russian strategic thinkers and practitioners are back 100-120 years in time, in the pre-World War I environment of ruthless strategic competition among the major powers.

Strategic Environment.

In the assessment of its professional military, Russia's external security environment has worsened since the break-up of the Soviet Union. The Russian Federation, they claim, finds itself in a dynamic and unstable neighborhood, with relations to a number of countries being tense, with tensions at times reaching dangerous levels. This is an amazing statement, which professes to minimize the dangers of Cold War confrontation and reveals the tenacity of traditional geopolitical thinking. Moscow's loss of ground in Central and Eastern Europe, the South Caucasus, and Central Asia is thus deemed more important than the gain in essentially nonadversarial relations with North Atlantic Treaty Organization (NATO) Europe and the countries of Northeast Asia. This, however, is consistent with the general view that demilitarization of relations with any country is a utopia. There can be no permanent friends.

This is not to say that Russian strategists do not value the current absence of military confrontation in Europe. They note with satisfaction the EU's general disinterest in building an integrated European military force and NATO's recent focus on Afghanistan. Moscow is, in principle, happy with the format of its relations with both the EU and NATO, which allows Russia to have a window on its neighbors and a possibility to raise any issue with them. It is very important that both relationships rest on the principle of equality and do not imply Russia's subordination to the powerful Euro-Atlantic institutions.

Strategic Loneliness.

Still, Russian leaders remain highly skeptical about the outlook for Russian-Western security cooperation, even though they admit a degree of commonality of interests. This conclusion is based on their reading of the results of the post-Cold War period during which they maintain the West took advantage of Russia's temporary weakness. "Interaction with the West has not enhanced Russia's military security," claimed General Staff Chief Yuri Baluevsky.

Vis-à-vis China, Russia enjoys a partnership relationship which it believes is its biggest strategic gain since 1991. Moscow has acknowledged China's rise and seeks to preserve an essentially equal relationship with its dynamic neighbor. However, Russian strategists recognize that an alliance with China, even if it were possible, would be Beijing rather than Moscow-led. More importantly, Russians remain ambivalent about the nature of the Sino-Russian relationship over the long term.

Moscow's nominal allies in the Collective Security Treaty Organization (CSTO) are either too weak (Kyrgyzstan), too self-centered (Armenia), or not loyal enough (Tajikistan). The remaining bigger CSTO members, Belarus and Kazakhstan, are increasingly independent-minded. Even though security relations with each of the CSTO countries are important in the relevant regional contexts, alliance relationships play a secondary and even tertiary role in Russia's strategic calculations. Basically, Russia is on its own, and alone. Its only true allies, just as 120 years ago, are its own

Army and Navy. Enhancing national military power is the overriding priority for the Kremlin.

The Principal Threat.

Russia's principal global concern is with U.S. foreign and security policy. Russian strategists see the United States as a *dangerous nation*, just like the title of Robert Kagan's most recent book. America, they reason, does not want a strong Russia, whom it fears as a potential strategic competitor, and thus resists its recovery and revival. U.S. policies and actions, especially in the areas of Russia's vital interests, i.e., Central Eurasia, are regarded as presenting a threat to Russia and its interests. This threat comes in various ways.

From the political perspective, Moscow believes that a decade and a half after the end of the Cold War, Washington still considers Russia an adversary, along with China and the rogue states, Iran and North Korea. It took recent remarks by Defense Secretary Robert Gates and Director of National Intelligence Mike McConnell as proof of that. Russian government analysts point to what they regard as an anti-Russian cabal in the Washington corridors of power involving members of Vice-President Dick Cheney's office, senior officials at the Departments of State and Defense, at the intelligence community, and on the Capitol Hill, on both sides of the aisle. They regard U.S. support for democracy in Russia as frankly subversive, and blame the U.S. media not only for anti-Russian bias, but more ominously for launching periodic campaigns of information warfare against Russia.

In geo-strategic terms, Moscow views with a wary eye the U.S. military presence near Russian borders. Since 2000, the United States has established bases in

Romania, Bulgaria, and Central Asia; sent military personnel to train and equip the Georgian military and exercised regularly with Ukrainian forces in Crimea and Western Ukraine. Further NATO enlargement, especially to include Georgia and Ukraine, would be regarded by Russian politico-military leaders as a clear provocation.

Since the mid-1990s, Russian strategic planners have noted U.S. propensity to use massive military force to achieve decisive political objectives. U.S./NATO bombings of the Bosnian Serbs first signaled the new trend, NATO's air war against Yugoslavia over Kosovo represented the watershed, and the invasion of Iraq confirmed it. Humanitarian interventions of the 1990s paved the way to preventive wars of choice in the 2000s. Moscow also realized that the United Nations (UN) Security Council, where it has a veto, and even the NATO alliance where several countries questioned U.S. policies, were not much of a constraint on the United States, which would bypass the UN and rely on the coalitions of the willing for a modicum of international legitimacy. Since 2005, Moscow U.S.-watchers have been expecting the United States to strike against Iran, destabilizing the situation south of Russian borders still further. As Russians have noted, all major U.S. military operations include a massive air campaign fought with precision-guided munitions and supported by sophisticated intelligence capabilities. From 2003, defending against an airspace attack has been officially designated as the principal task of the Russian Armed Forces.

Moscow has noticed U.S. disdain for arms control agreements. The George W. Bush administration's withdrawal from the Anti-Ballistic Missile (ABM) Treaty and its initial unwillingness to proceed with strategic arms reductions were interpreted as reflecting a U.S. desire to be fully unbound. U.S. plans to construct ballistic missile defense (BMD) sites in Central Europe are deemed to be part of a global plan to achieve strategic superiority over Russia: Iran, the Russians maintain, is only camouflage. Russia watches U.S. military programs with alarm in regard to outer space and perfecting nuclear weapons and their employment strategies. In particular, Russian strategists point to U.S. efforts aimed at miniaturizing nuclear weapons which would then become usable on the battlefield. Last, but not least, Russians believe the United States would use their weakness to its advantage. NATO enlargement and the fate of the Conventional Armed Forces in Europe (CFE) Treaty are cited as examples. It follows that no promises or assurances from the United States should be accepted at face value.

Other Threats.

Though U.S. policies remain Russia's principal strategic concern and a potential central threat, Russian security is more immediately affected by other factors. Moreover, in a number of cases Russian and U.S./Western interests coincide to a significant extent, thus creating a foundation for collaboration. There are shooting wars along the perimeter of Russia's borders. Moscow does not object to U.S./NATO military presence in Afghanistan. Immediately after September 11, 2001 (9/11), Russia and the United States cooperated closely to remove the Taliban from power in Afghanistan. The 2001 U.S.-led operation, assisted by Russia, removed the most serious external threat to Russia's security. Moscow has been willing to "assign" Afghanistan to the U.S./NATO zone of responsibility, but it is increasingly uncertain about the length and depth of the Western commitment to the security of that country. It fears a collapse of the Western effort and a return of the Taliban.

A much more threatening prospect would be destabilization of Central Asia. This could result from either of two sources: an outpouring of Islamist radicalism from a Taliban-ruled Afghanistan, or an Islamist-led domestic uprising in a Central Asian country against the authorities. The latter, in the Russian view, might well be the result of U.S.-sponsored democracy promotion, undermining the legitimacy of the secular authoritarians.

The war in Iraq, from the Russian perspective, harbors the threat of releasing into the neighborhood and beyond thousands of hardened and experienced jihadists. Some of these people could find their way into Russia's North Caucasus and into Central Asia, threatening the precarious status quo there. Another danger of a deteriorating situation in Iraq lies in the prospect of a military showdown between the United States and Iran. Even though some elements in Russia might relish at the prospect of the United States becoming ever deeper bogged down in the Middle East, and in particular over the likely jump in oil prices, such a war would have the tremendous downside of radicalizing Russia's southern neighborhood. It would also lead to a sharp political division, even alienation, between Moscow and Washington, far beyond where the Russians would feel it safe to go.

The issue of weapons of mass destruction (WMD) proliferation, at the heart of the U.S.-Iranian dispute, is recognized by Russians as both real and serious, but not immediate or necessarily catastrophic. Moscow generally prefers to deal with individual cases of WMD proliferation with the use of political, not military, instruments. From the Russian perspective, India has never been a problem, though Pakistan was and is. Israel's deterrent is of existential matter and has been in place for decades. The North Korean regime, though not given much sympathy in the Kremlin, is believed to be resorting to nuclear and missile blackmail not only as a means of procuring much-needed resources, but as a security policy in view of U.S. policies of regime change. Iran, as a major regional player, is a more serious case, the Russians believe, and it needs to be managed politically on a quid pro quo basis.

As Russia claims to be an energy superpower, its strategists regard as threats any actions that would deny it access to energy resources or block transit of Russian natural gas and oil. Russians also take a dim view of calls to create an "energy NATO," which would unite European energy consumers under U.S. leadership and offer protection to those member states that may have energy disputes with Russia.

Russia has the world's longest land borders. When the Soviet Union broke apart, much of their length was not enshrined in treaties. Of the agreements concluded since then, the several treaties with China stand out. President Vladimir Putin regards finalizing the Russo-Chinese border along its entire length as one of his most important foreign policy achievements. By contrast, the territorial issue with Japan has remained unresolved. Russian strategists count current and potential territorial claims on Russia, including in the Arctic, among the more relevant threats to its national security.

The frozen conflicts in the former Soviet space, Transnistria, Abkhazia, South Ossetia, and Nagorno-Karabakh, are fraught with the danger of new violence.

In such an event, Russia will become immediately involved due to its military presence as peacekeeper in the first three conflict areas, as the principal patron of the unrecognized states, and also because most Abkhazians and South Ossetians, as well as many Transnistrians, hold Russian passports. Moscow's concerns are of two kinds. One is that Russia is provoked into a military response, especially by Georgia, which would transform small ethnic conflicts into a full-blown interstate one, with the West rallying behind Tbilisi. The other concern is that the current nonperforming formula for peaceful resolution, which places Russia into the dominant position, is replaced by a multilateral format in which Western institutions, such as NATO, will play the leading role.

During much of Russia's post-Soviet history, its forces were engaged in the conflict in Chechnya. By the mid-2000s, hostilities in Chechnya had died down. Putin's policy of *Chechenization* has worked. Still, the North Caucasus remains a locus of volatility and insecurity, with separatism and terrorism continuing as threats to the stability of the Russian Federation. From the Kremlin's perspective, Western public condemnation of Russian actions in Chechnya and the granting of asylum to several separatist leaders testify to the Western interest in weakening and destabilizing Russia.

Finally, Russian strategists recognize the importance of information warfare, and not only with reference to the Western media. They are particularly concerned with the spread of radical Islamist propaganda that may affect the loyalties of the growing Muslim community in the Russian Federation.

Policy Implications.

Russia's policies are not, at least not yet, anti-American. Having rejected U.S. tutelage, Moscow is not willing to become a junior partner to China. Rather, its strategists and policymakers see Russia on a par with both America and China, as one of the world's principal independent strategic actors. The global strategic situation is still fluid, with no firm dividing lines. With Washington, Moscow seeks a relationship that would be based on equality, a kind of partnership through strength. Failing that "new deal," Russia would have to brace itself for strategic rivalry and competition, combined with cooperation in a limited number of areas.

Russian strategists expect the EU to remain incoherent for some time and have discounted it as a strategic factor in Europe. They have similarly discounted NATO, whose focus has shifted to Afghanistan. From Moscow's perspective, the country to watch in Europe is the United States, which reaches out in particular to Moscow's former Warsaw Pact allies and Commonwealth of Independent States (CIS) partners, who bear grudges against Russia.

Moscow has made bolstering its strategic deterrence capability a major priority. The nuclear triad will be maintained, and its elements modernized. Having managed to stabilize, albeit at a fairly low level, its conventional forces, the Russian leadership now prepares to start its first post-Soviet modernization and rearmament program. This effort is likely to be substantial, but modest by comparison to the Soviet programs of the 1970s and 1980s. Russia will have more contract soldiers, but will keep conscription and a scaled-down mobilization base for a large-scale war which its strategists refuse to rule out. At this juncture, the Kremlin is primarily concerned with keeping tight control over the money flows within the defense establishment. As the defense industrial base is being slowly revived, it is also being restructured. Aerospace, shipbuilding, and defense exports have been designated as the key sectors.

Moscow can be expected to work actively against NATO enlargement to include Georgia and Ukraine. It will appeal to diverse interests inside NATO in an effort to derail or constrain those developments, such as NATO enlargement and BMD deployments, which it sees as detrimental to its security. It will continue to press for complete U.S. military withdrawal from Central Asia.

Russia is starting to rethink arms control. The Kremlin is leaning to terminate Russia's participation in the treaties which have outlived their usefulness or constrain Moscow's efforts to provide for national security. This concerns primarily the CFE and Intermediate Range Nuclear Forces (INF) treaties concluded, respectively, in 1990 and 1987. Russia, however, has not lost interest in arms control. It would be ready to negotiate new, but more comprehensive, agreements, i.e., including other countries besides NATO members and itself, and on an equal footing. Otherwise, the Kremlin would prefer a freedom of hands.

Moscow's alliances policy has a very limited place in the overall strategy. It sees little use in permanent arrangements. The CSTO is not a Warsaw Pact II. The Russian Armed Forces aim for full strategic and operational self-sufficiency, even as they exercise with CSTO and Shanghai Cooperation Organization (SCO) partners and seek to develop interoperability with NATO.

Chechnya and the North Caucasus remain the Kremlin's most immediate security concern. Chechenization, or better said, Kadyrovization, can only be a temporary solution. Even though Moscow has learned that only Muslims can control Muslims, it is still far from restoring stability to its vulnerable southern flank. With regard to Central Asia, Russia will continue to bolster the local regimes, and seek to engage them more closely bilaterally and within the CSTO. The Russians have concluded that democracy promotion does not bring liberals to power, but can help Islamist radicals to topple secular authoritarians and create instability. In Afghanistan, should NATO fail, Russia will probably fall back to supporting its friends in the former Northern Alliance; if they fail, it would have to either cut deals with the Taliban, or seek new ways of opposing them. The lesson Moscow learned in Afghanistan says that yesterday's enemy can turn out to be a friend, and vice versa.

Russian leaders see the situation in Iraq as hopeless for the United States, and prepare for the consequences of that major failure of the U.S. policy, in particular, an influx of jihadists. With reference to Iran, Moscow will continue to plead for a political solution, but above all will stay out of the fray. The Kremlin fears that taking on a major Islamic power would provoke a clash of civilizations, including within countries with sizeable Muslim minorities, as in Russia. Russia's preferred option would be to wait for internal moderate forces in Iran to mature and work from within to mellow a recalcitrant regime.

Russia keeps a wary eye on Pakistan, where internal destabilization and Islamist radicalization cannot be ruled out.

Last, but not least, there is China. From Moscow's perspective, good-neighborly relations with the Asian giant are a must. Right now, the relationship is good, with economic exchanges growing. Politically, China and Russia are partners in Central Asia; they also want an end to U.S. global dominance. The still thriving arms relationship is important for both countries. Moscow is highly allergic to real or perceived U.S. attempts to undermine its partnership with Beijing. Yet, there are real constraints on that partnership, including latent fears on both sides.

Russian strategic planners believe that China will not present a major threat to Russia at least for the next 15-20 years. By 2020-30, Russia hopes to have fully recovered, sufficiently developed its eastern provinces, and modernized its military, providing it with effective deterrence capabilities. By that time, China and the United States can be expected to be the world's principal strategic competitors, keenly focused on each other. Rather than being sandwiched between two superpowers, Russia hopes to be a major independent actor and maybe even an arbiter between the two.

BIOGRAPHICAL SKETCHES OF THE AUTHORS

R. CRAIG NATION has been Professor of Strategy and Director of Russian and Eurasian Studies at the U.S. Army War College since 1996. He specializes in security affairs with a special emphasis upon the European and Eurasian areas. He has taught History and International Relations at Duke University, the University of Southern California, Cornell University, and The Johns Hopkins University School of Advanced International Studies. Professor Nation earned his Ph.D. in Contemporary History from Duke University.

DMITRI TRENIN is a senior associate of the Carnegie Endowment, the deputy director of the Carnegie Moscow Center and chair of its Foreign and Security Policy Program. He has been with the Center since its inception in 1993. From 1993-97, Mr. Trenin held posts as a senior research fellow at the NATO Defense College in Rome, a visiting professor at the Free University of Brussels and a senior research fellow at the Institute of Europe in Moscow. He served in the Soviet and Russian armed forces from 1972 to 1993, including experience working as a liaison officer in the External Relations Branch of the Group of Soviet Forces Germany and as a staff member of the delegation to the U.S.-Soviet nuclear arms talks in Geneva from 1985 to 1991. He also taught at the Defense University in Moscow. Mr. Trenin authored *Getting Russia Right* (2007, forthcoming); *Russia's Restless Frontier: The Chechnya Factor in Post-Soviet Russia* (2004; with Aleksei V. Malashenko) and *The End of Eurasia: Russia on the Border Between Geopolitics and Globalization*, (2001). He edited, with Steven Miller, *The Russian Military: Power and Policy* (2006).

Lightning Source UK Ltd.
Milton Keynes UK
UKHW010131061021
391693UK00002B/384